FACTS from SCIENCE

OM KIDZ

An imprint of Om Books International

Contents

The Big Bang 4

The Solar System, Formation of Earth 6

Heavenly Bodies 8

Man Goes to Space 10

Matter 12

Particles of Matter 14

Reactions 16

Radioactivity 18

Electricity 20

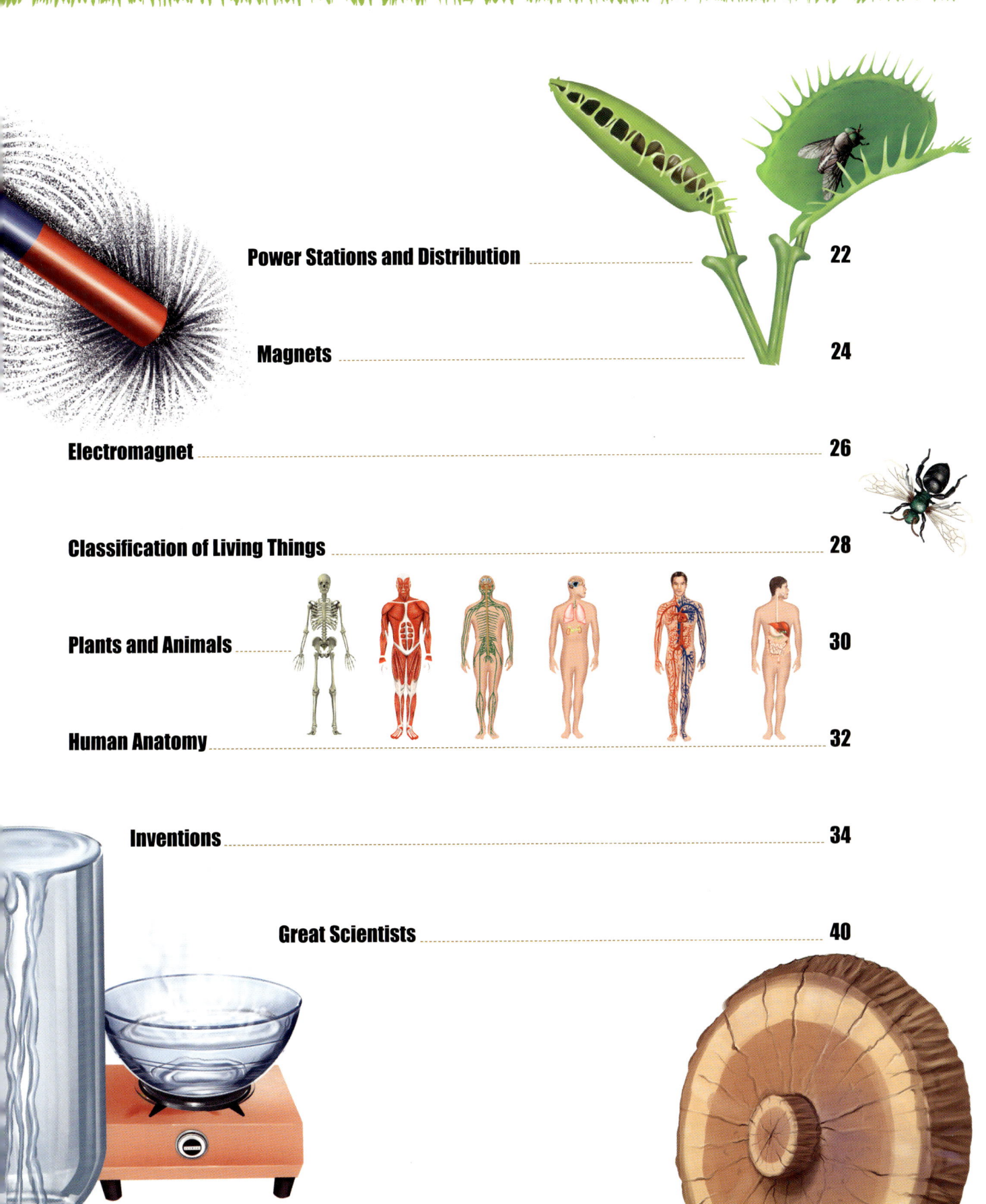

Power Stations and Distribution 22

Magnets 24

Electromagnet 26

Classification of Living Things 28

Plants and Animals 30

Human Anatomy 32

Inventions 34

Great Scientists 40

The Big Bang

Scientists believe that the universe began about 15 billion years ago. It was as small as a needle head. Soon it started to expand very fast. It was so fast that it seemed like an explosion. This sudden explosive growth is called the Big Bang. The theory of the Big Bang was first penned down by a Russian and a Belgian scientist — Alexender Friedmann and Abbe Georges Lemaitre, respectively.

Stage 1

The needle head universe suddenly started expanding like an explosion. Great flashes of light and heat were generated. It became a very hot bowl of electrons and other particles.

▼ *Stage 1*   ▼ *Stage 2*

Stage 2

Slowly, in the next million years, the cluster of particles started to clear-up and the cooling process also got initiated. Many tiny particles combined together and filled most of the universe with Hydrogen and Helium gases.

Stage 3

It took the next billion years to unite the Hydrogen and Helium gases to form giant masses of clouds and thus galaxies were formed. Smaller clusters of these clouds collapsed and the first stars were born.

Stage 4

After 15 billion years of the Big Bang, gravity united various clusters of galaxies which contained billions of stars. Space dust united together and formed planets. Earth is one of these planets.

▼ Stage 3   ▼ Stage 4

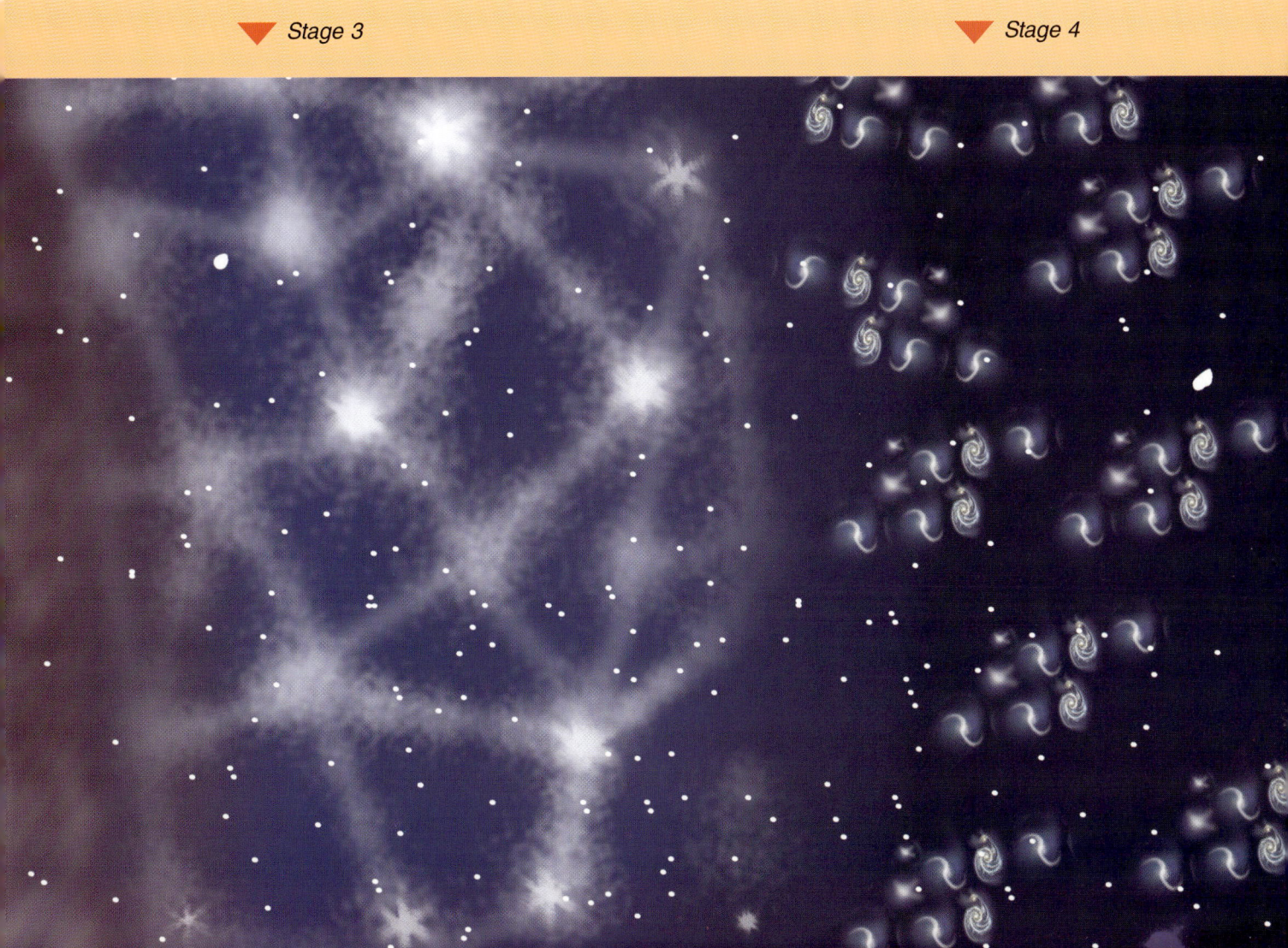

The Solar System

The Solar System consists of the Sun and its main eight planets. Most of these planets have their natural satellites, which are called their Moons. Apart from the Sun, the planets and their moons, the Solar System also consists of billions of other bodies like asteroids, comets, meteoroids and space dust.

It is believed that more than 4 billion years ago a giant cloud of dust, gases and other particles collapsed. These particles and gases reunited in clusters under the gravitational pull of each other and formed planets. Now they revolve around the Sun in their orbits. They are all bound around the Sun because of its (Sun's) gravity.

Mercury is the closest and the smallest planet around the Sun. Venus is the hottest planet in the Solar System. Earth is the only planet known to consist of living beings. Like Earth, Mars also has volcanoes and has a red coloured soil, which is basically the rust in its iron rich soil. Jupiter is the largest planet in the

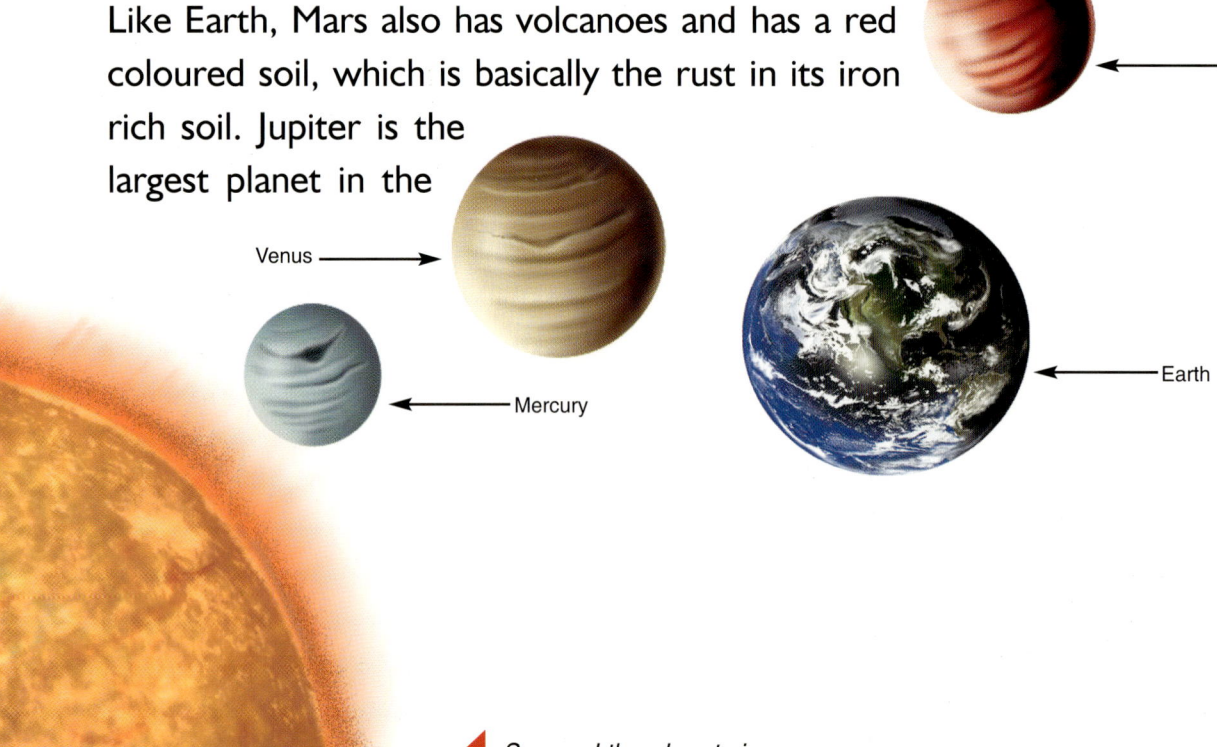

◀ *Sun and the planets in sequence*

Solar System and is mostly made up of gases. Saturn is popularly known to have a ring around it. This ring is mainly made of dust particles. Uranus is the lightest planet of the outer core and radiates the least heat into space. Neptune is 17 times more massive than Earth and radiates more heat into space. Originally classified as a planet, Pluto is now considered as the second largest dwarf planet in the Solar System, and a part of the Kulper belt.

Eris

It is the largest known dwarf planet in the Solar System till now. It is approximately 27% more massive than Pluto.

◀ *This is how dust became the Earth*

There were huge amounts of dust and gases around the Sun. They clumped together to form planetesimals, and slowly they became larger and cooled down to form planets. One of them was the Earth.

Heavenly Bodies

There are various objects suspended throughout the universe. These are often called the Heavenly Bodies. The most popular and common Heavenly Bodies then are Stars, Comets, Galaxies, and Constellations.

Stars

Stars are masses of Hydrogen and Helium gases. A star glows because there is a kind of reaction in the core, like those in nuclear bombs, that generates a huge amount of light and heat. The smaller the star the larger its life. The life of a small star is said to be upto 200 billion years whereas a mid-size star lasts for about 10 billion years. The Sun is a mid-size star.

Comets

A comet is basically a huge mass of dust and ice revolving on its extremely large orbit around the Sun (not all comets revolve around Sun but mostly do). Their orbits are so big that most of the times they are far away from the Sun. But when they come near the Sun the ice starts melting and disintegrates from the mass. And the moment the light from the Sun falls on it, we see a glowing tail of the comet. The most famous comet known to all of us is the Hailey's comet.

Galaxy

Galaxies are huge groups of billions of stars. They are often found in groups called clusters. It is believed that there are trillions of galaxies in the whole universe. Galaxies are found mainly in three shapes: Spiral, Elliptical and Irregular.

Constellations

Constellations are a group of stars that form a pattern or a figure. These figures are formed and agreed upon by the astronomers to identify a group or individual stars. These stars actually don't have any relationship in between and are several thousand miles apart. The brightest star in a constellation is known as Alpha. It is said that astronomers today have already discovered more than 80 constellations.

Nebula

These are bodies formed by clouds of various gases and space dust. Lot of them give off a glowing effect as the hydrogen gas in them gets heated off from the space radiations. Though there are glowing nebulae, we also find dark nebulae in space which absorb all light.

Man Goes to Space

Yuri Gagarin was the first astronaut from Russia to go to space. Russians call their space pilots cosmonauts. Yuri Gagarin, way back in April 1961, made his first journey to space. Later in 1969 Neil Armstrong from America made the giant leap for mankind and set foot on the moon. This was the year when a human being stepped on the moon for the first time. With the help of a Laser beam and a mirror placed on the moon, man enabled itself to also calculate the distance between the Earth and the moon. It is a surprising 376275 kms. Do you know you can jump 7 times higher on the moon than on Earth? It is because the gravity of the moon is much less than that of Earth. The temperature on the moon can fall down to -160°C at night.

▲ A spacecraft

Spacesuit

Astronauts need to wear a spacesuit as soon as they leave the spacecraft. A spacesuit is designed to replicate the Earth's atmospheric conditions. It presses us down from inside and gives us fresh air to breathe. It has water tube linings inside to keep our body at the right temperature. The outer layer of the spacesuit is designed to protect us from harmful radiations and super-speedy micrometeoroids. A very sturdy helmet is designed to protect the astronaut against any dangerous radiation and space dust particles.

◄ Man wearing a spacesuit

Spacecraft

A manned spacecraft is made up of two important sections. One is the astronaut section and the other is the equipment section. The astronaut section has all the instruments to control the spacecraft. It has special windows which protect against any kind of harmful radiations from coming. Besides, this is where the astronauts sleep, eat and also freshen up. The equipment section has the life support system, the power supply, engine and the fuel.

Life support system is the system which supplies fresh air (a mixture of Oxygen and Nitrogen) to the crew. It also removes the Carbon-dioxide with the help of special pellets and also maintains the right temperature and humidity inside the compartment. A reusable spacecraft is called a space shuttle.

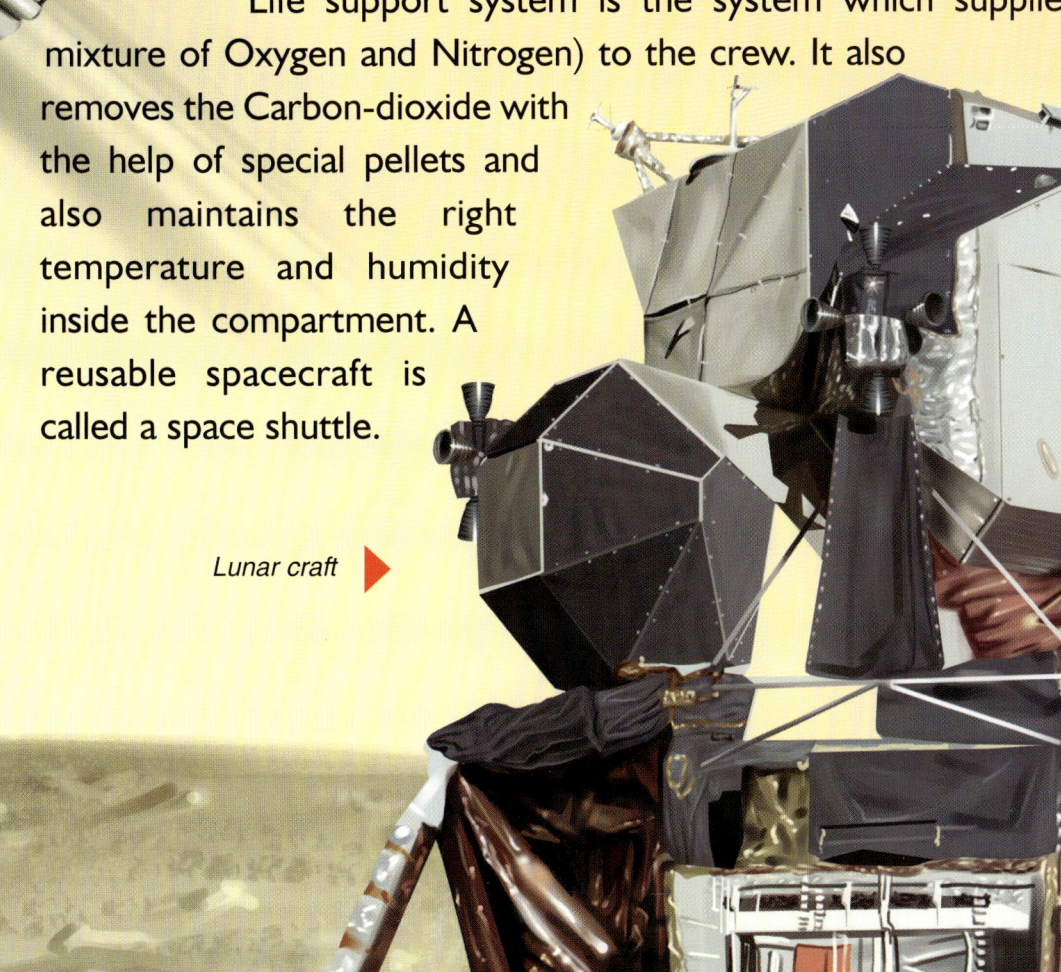

Lunar craft ▶

Matter

Matter is what the whole universe is made up of. One can say that every physical state is made up of matter. Starting from this page, the air you breathe, the liquids that you drink, everything is made up of matter. There are basically three states of matter — solid, liquid and gas. The state of a matter is defined by the kind of bonding the molecules in it has. Most of the matter can exist in any state depending on the temperature.

▼ *Solid*

Solid

In solids, the molecules are tightly bound with each other and cannot move easily at all. That is the reason a solid object does not change its shape so easily and has a definite physical appearance. An example of solid matter is diamond.

Liquid

Liquids do not have any fixed shape and often take the shape of the container they are in. This is because the molecules in the liquid are loosely held together. In a liquid, the molecules move around each other, hence enabling the matter to flow as in the case of water.

Gas

Unlike solids and liquids, in gases, molecules are not held together at all. This enables a gas to fill any container evenly. And if you open up the container, the moving molecules escape into the open area. Because of such free and loose molecules, it is difficult to even touch and feel a gaseous matter.

▼ Liquid

▼ Gas

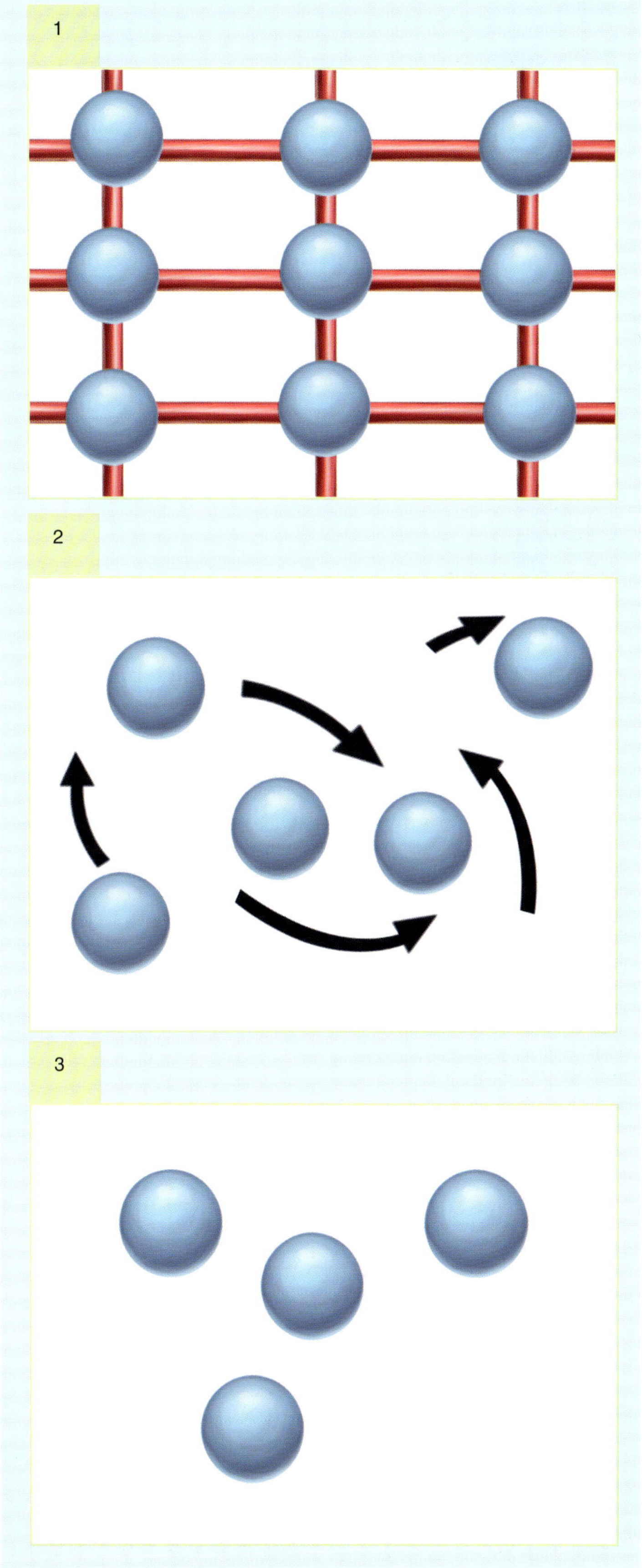

1

2

3

1. Diagram showing the molecules in a solid object. Here the molecules are held tightly with each other and have almost no scope to move around.

2. This diagram shows how the molecules of a liquid substance are placed around each other. Here molecules are loosely bound and move around each other much freely than in solid objects.

3. This diagram shows that molecules move around freely to the level that they can almost escape in the atmosphere or can simply fill up any enclosed volume.

Particles of Matter

Atom

Atoms are primarily made up of three main particles: Proton, Neutron and Electron. Protons and Neutrons are found in the Nucleus and Electrons revolve around in their orbits around the Nucleus. Neutrons have no charge, whereas Protons are positively charged and Electrons are negatively charged. The number of Protons and Electrons in an atom are always the same. As they are of opposite charges, they attract each other. This is why an Electron stays in its orbit around the Nucleus.

Element

An Element is made up of atoms with identical number of protons in each of its nucleii. Elements cannot be further broken to form a simpler substance by normal chemical means. Our environment, such as air and water, constitutes of many such elements. For example, the Oxygen that we breathe is an element. Pure Iron or Copper are also elements. They fall under the metal group.

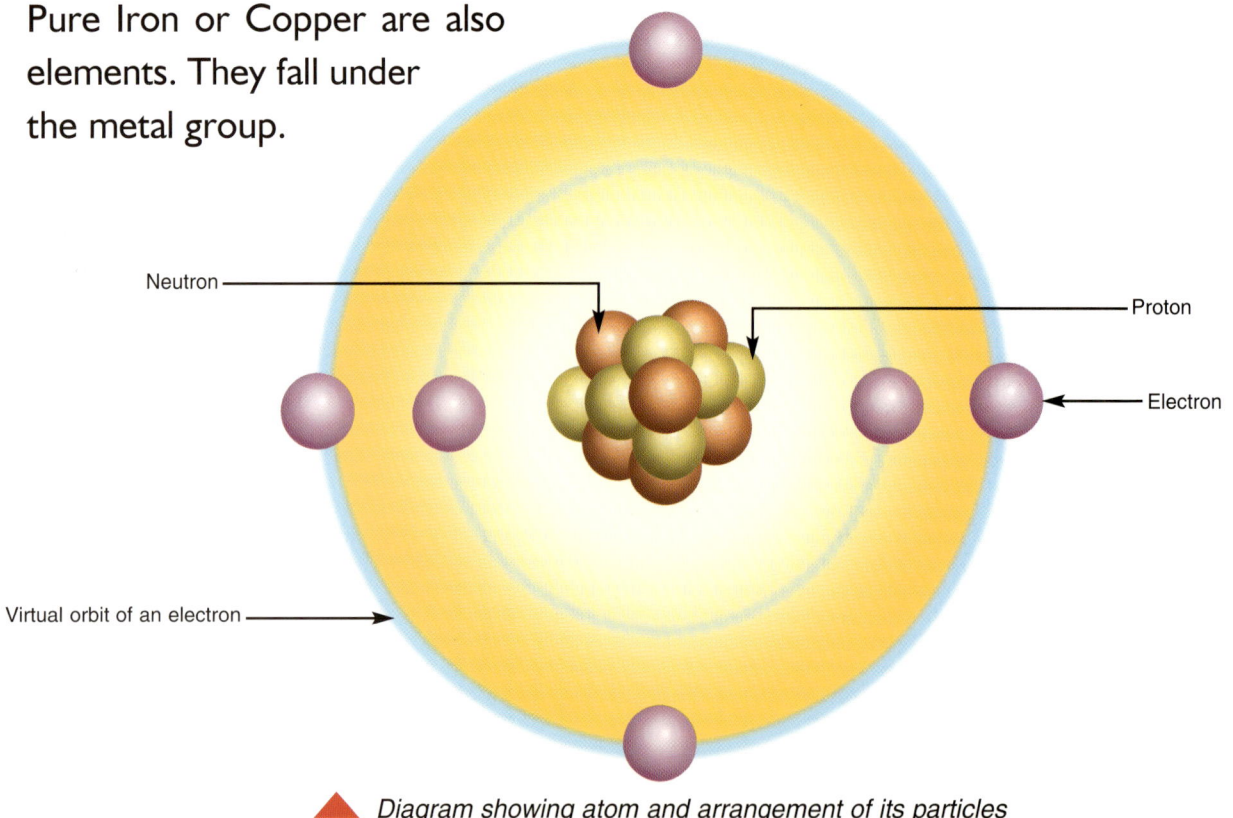

▲ Diagram showing atom and arrangement of its particles

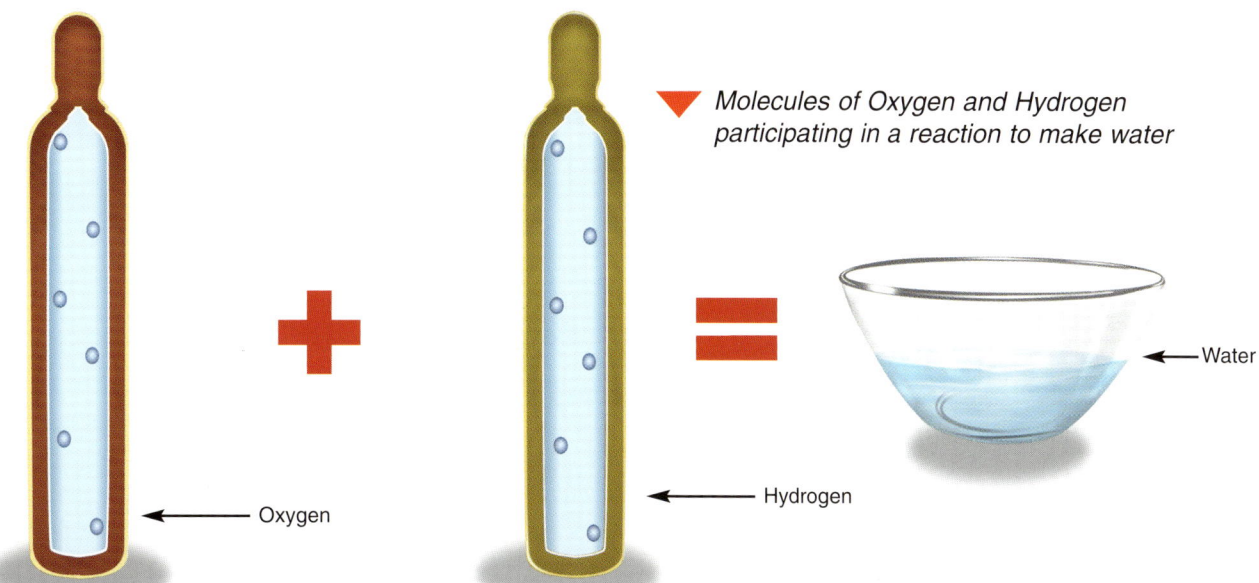

Molecules of Oxygen and Hydrogen participating in a reaction to make water

Molecule

A group of two or more atoms composed together defining the chemical or physical state of a substance (for example solid, liquid or gas) is called a Molecule. These are the smallest part of a compound that can participate in a reaction to create a change in the physical and chemical property of the very substance. For example: molecules of Oxygen and molecules of Hydrogen participate in a particular reaction and water is formed.

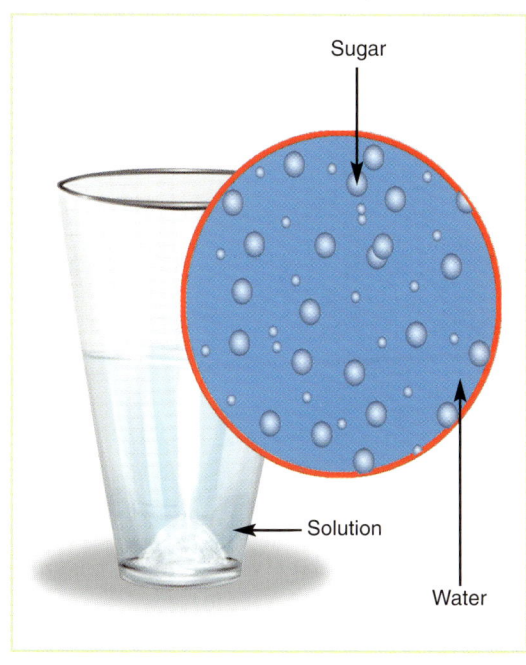

Compound

Let us take the same example of Oxygen and Hydrogen. Oxygen and Hydrogen both are gases. When combined together under certain circumstances they become water, which is a liquid. Water is a compound. Hence a compound is the unification of 2 or more elements through a reaction. A compound might have an absolute different physical and chemical property than that of the elements that are used to create it.

Reactions

Scientifically the most common and studied reactions are the Chemical Reactions. It is a process that results in interconversion of different substances. The substances involved in these kind of reactions are called Reactants. These reactants react under a given circumstance and undergo a chemical change. The results often produce one or more compounds, which are absolutely of different nature to those of the reactants.

Let us take a very common example. We take two substances: wood and fresh air. Wood is fuel and fresh air is Oxygen. We make the environment around the wood

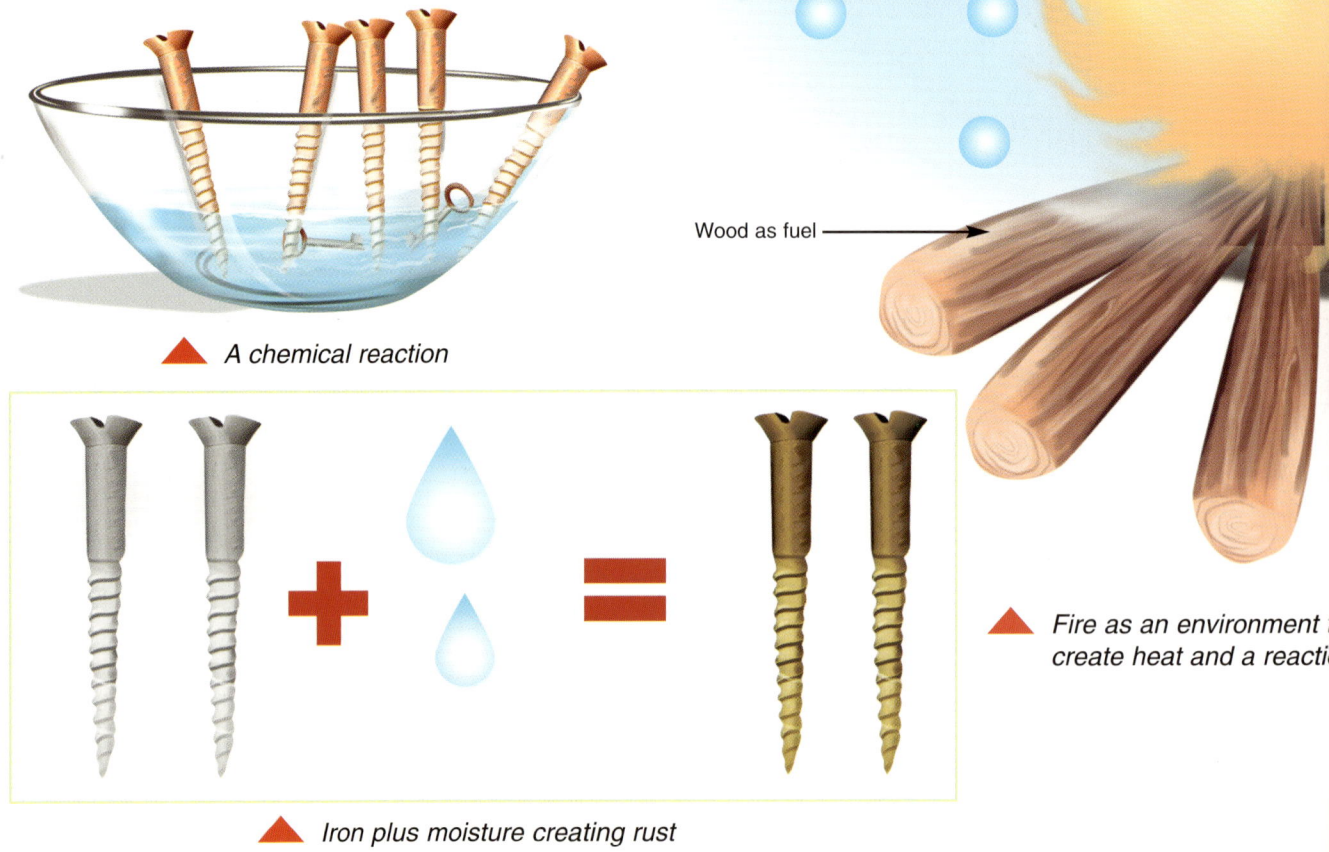

▲ A chemical reaction

▲ Iron plus moisture creating rust

▲ Fire as an environment create heat and a reaction

- Charcoal
- Choking greyish fumes
- Unburnt particles and carbon

very hot by lighting up a fire. The wood starts burning. After it is completely burnt, we get a grayish black ash and choking grayish fumes. Now wood is solid brown and fresh air is transparent and easy to breathe. But after the reaction, at the end, we get grayish black ash which is different from wood and the choking fumes which is totally opposite to the fresh air we breathe. Therefore, wood + oxygen = fly ash + Carbon-dioxide + unburnt particles.

Another example is iron screws reacting with water and air. The solid shining iron screws when react with moist air turn into rusty brittle substance.

▲ Sodium   ▲ Chlorine liquid   ▲ Salt

Radioactivity

▲ Hans Geiger

When an element does not change its characteristics without an external force acting on it, it is called a stable element. But all elements are not stable. The nucleii of these elements are continuously breaking down and emitting particles to become stable. This phenomenon of shedding particles and trying to get stable is called Radioactivity. The particles emitted are generally categorised as alpha, beta and gamma. When one element sheds these particles, most of the times they also turn into other elements, like Plutonium breaks and becomes Uranium and through its further breaking Thorium is created.

▲ Geiger counter

▶ Scientists digging out bones of extinct animals for carbon dating

Carbon Dating

All the living things on Earth contain a special form of Carbon in the body. Now this Carbon starts decaying when the living thing dies. Scientists have discovered that the nucleus of this Carbon takes 5,730 years to get half dead or to come to its half life. By calculating the amount of this Carbon left or decayed, scientists can fairly say the time period of when a particular dead living thing existed. This whole process is called Carbon Dating.

Half Life

It is the time needed for a nucleus of any radioactive substance to undergo a decay and reduce to half of its initial weight. For example, if a radioactive substance has a half life of 1 minute and its weight is 10 grams then after 30 seconds only 5 grams should be left and after the next 15 seconds only 2.5 grams, and so on till it perishes. Because a particular element has a certain number of neutrons and protons, therefore, as they shed off these particles they change to other elements. (As in the case of Plutonium breaking into Uranium.)

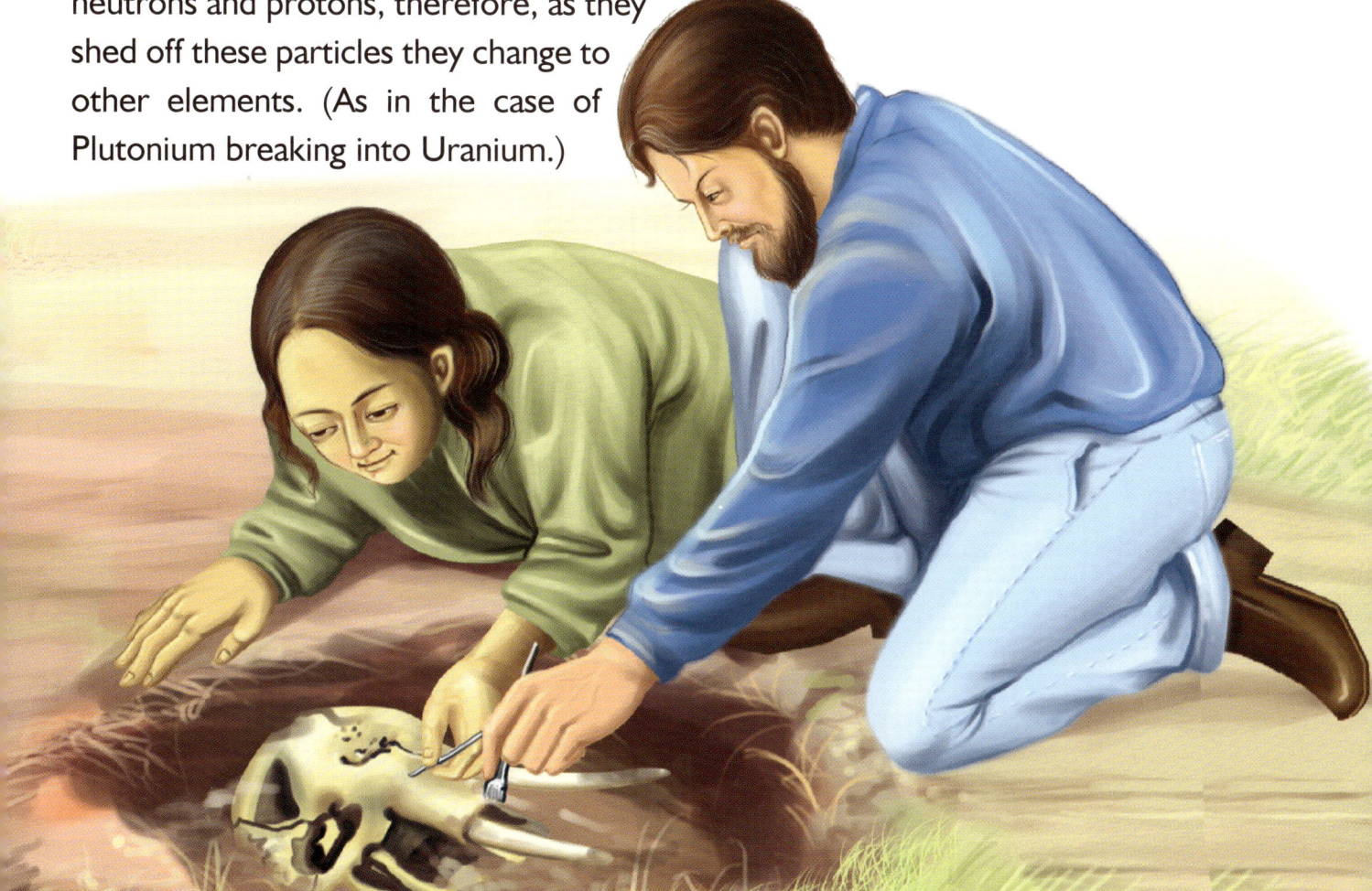

Electricity

Electricity is a kind of energy produced due to the movement of a negatively charged particle of an atom. This negatively charged particle is called Electron. We already know that number of electrons is equal to number of protons in a nucleus which is positively charged. Therefore, when an electron moves to stabilize itself, this movement causes electricity. An Italian scientist Alessandro Volta was known to be the pioneer of electricity. Therefore, electricity is measured in 'Volts'.

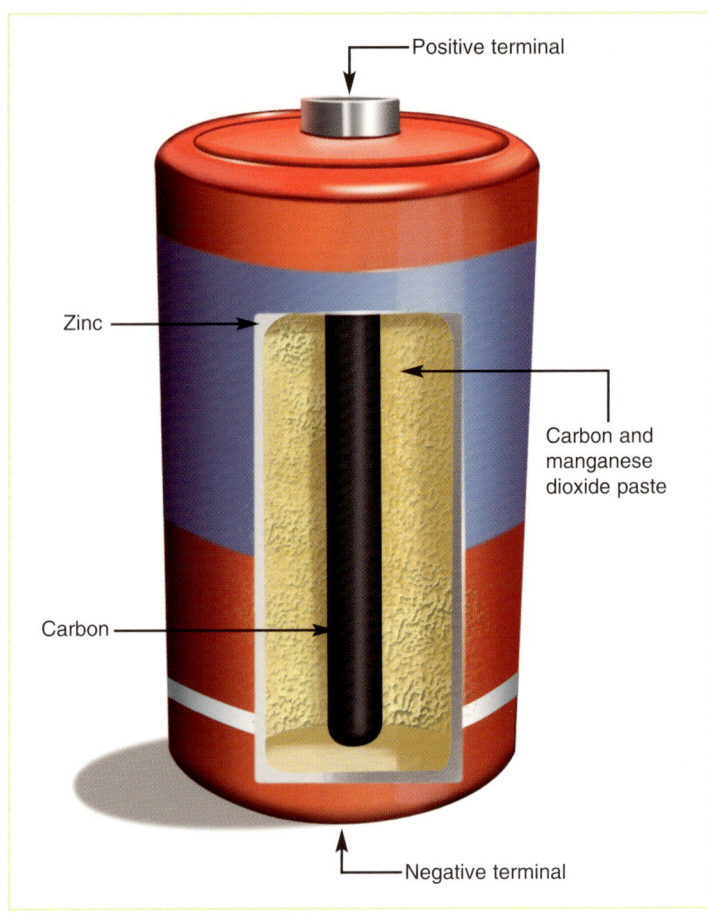

▲ *A domestic battery*

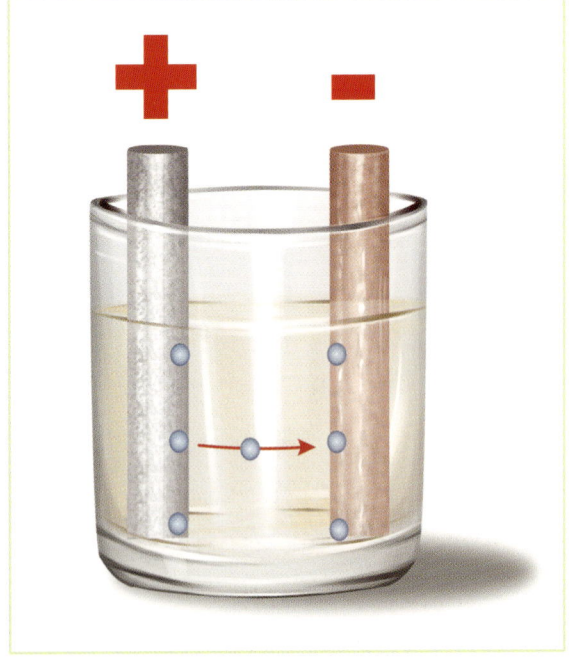

▲ *Movement of electrons, creating current*

Battery

Alessandro Volta also invented the first battery. A battery is designed in such a way that one end produces and loses electrons and the other end gains electrons. The end that loses electrons becomes the negative terminal and the one which gains becomes the positive terminal. The modern day torch battery is a composition of Carbon and Zinc reactions.

Resistance is a very common phenomenon in any electrical circuit. It is the ability of a material to resist the flow of electrons (electrical current). To resist this flow a special type of component is developed and is called Resistor. George Ohm discovered this process and thus the resistance is measured in 'Ohms'.

Capacitor

It is a device developed to store electrical charges. It basically consists of special plates separated in between by an insulator. This ability of storing charges by a capacitor is called Capacitance.

Integrated Circuit (IC)

The word IC came from Integrated Circuits. It is a miniature version of a very complicated circuit. ICs are semiconductor Wafers on which many micro resistors, capacitors and transistors are fabricated to obtain a certain result.

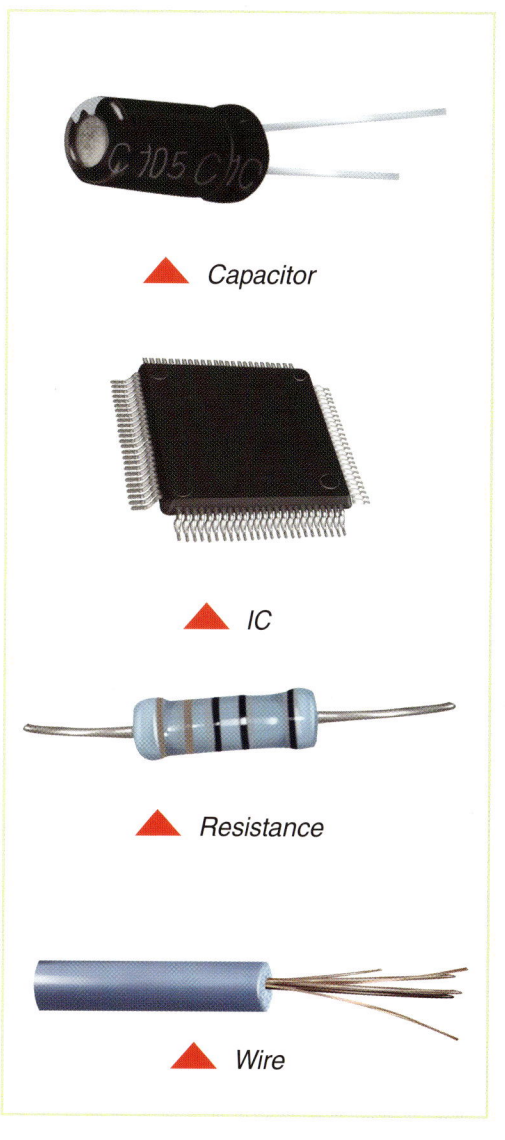

▲ *Capacitor*

▲ *IC*

▲ *Resistance*

▲ *Wire*

Circuit

An electrical design that enables the current (electrons) to flow from one point to another point, is known as a circuit. Every circuit is designed to achieve a particular result.

◀ *A conventional circuit*

21

Power Stations and Distribution

A Power Station is a place where various kinds of fuels are used and the energy produced by them is transmitted to the generator which in turn produces consistent electricity for the people. There are basically three kinds of power stations.

Thermal Power Station

It is a power station that uses fossil fuels such as coal, charcoal to produce electricity. Till now, most of the electricity generated in the world is through thermal power stations.

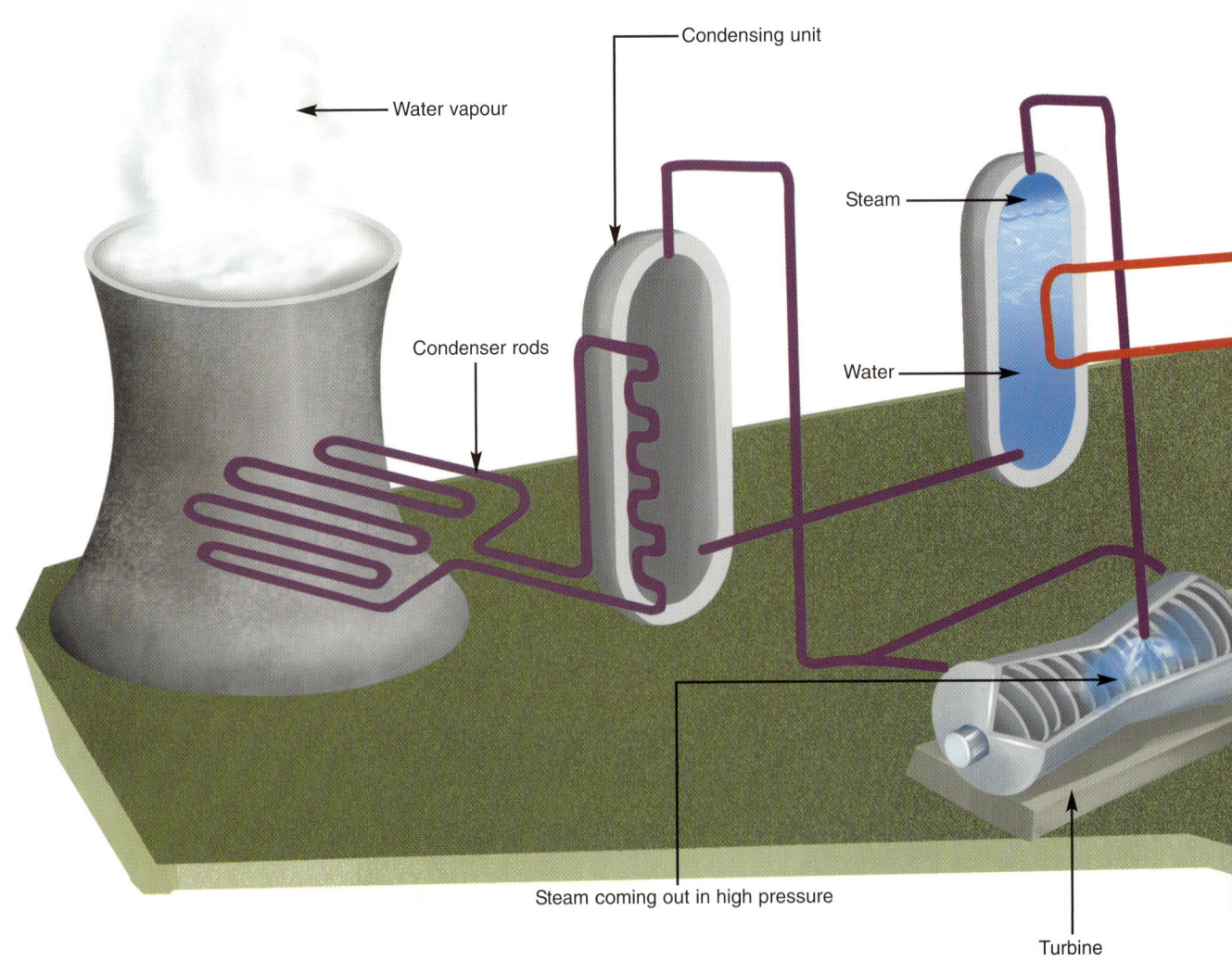

Hydro Power Stations

This kind of station uses the sheer power of the natural water resources available and converts the water power into electricity through the generators. These stations are found mainly in mountains or places with plenty of natural water resources.

Nuclear Power Stations

These power stations use special elements such as Uranium to produce heat energy which is later converted into electrical energy through generators.

▼ *Nuclear power station*

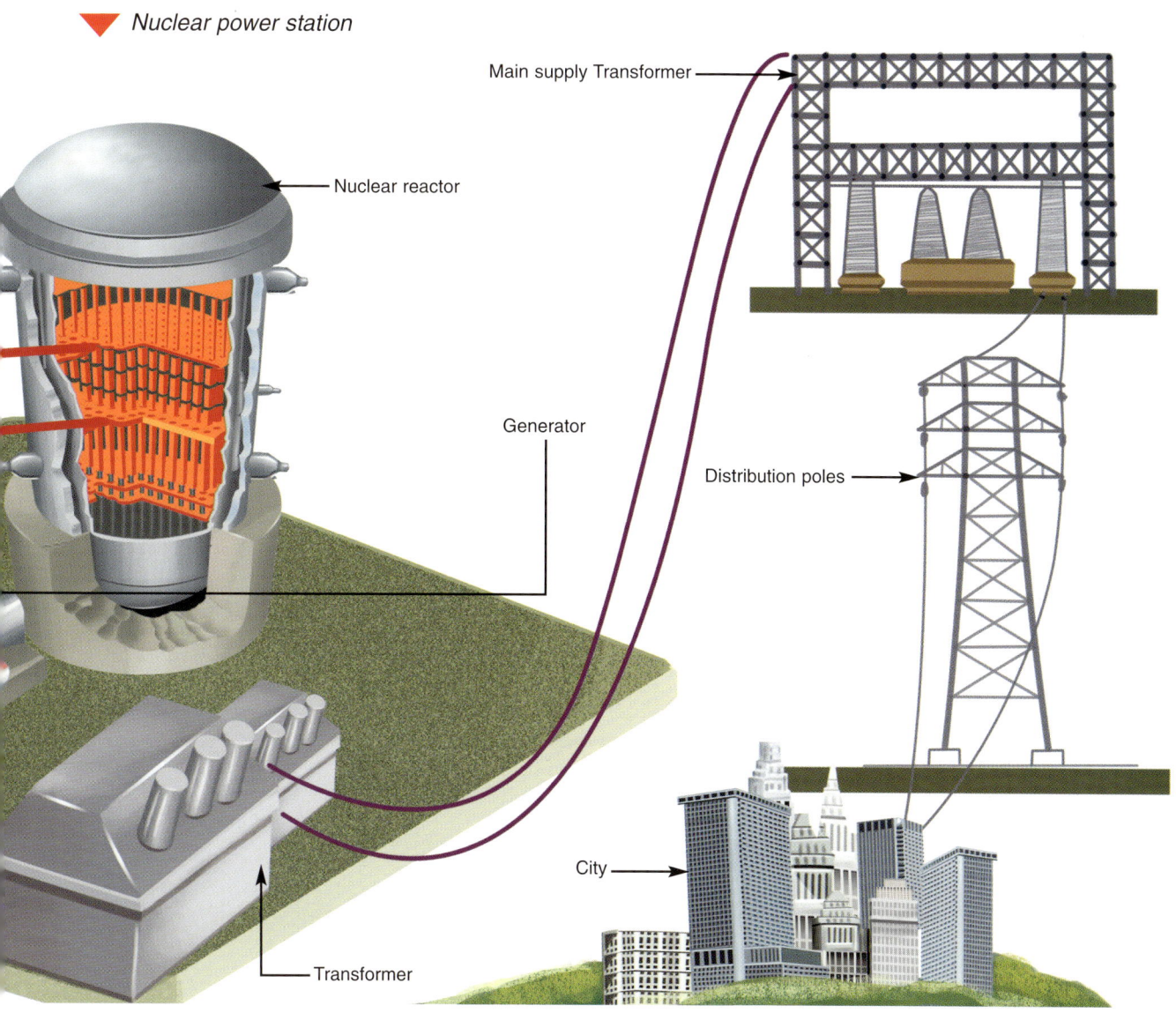

Magnets

A Magnet is a type of object which produces a magnetic field. Magnets have a surprising ability to attract few metal objects, mainly Iron. All magnets have two poles, one is the north pole and the other is the south pole. Opposite poles attract each other, whereas similar poles repel each other.

▶ *A horse shoe magnet attracting metal objects*

Magnetic Field

It is an invisible line of force around a magnet which connects the north pole with the south pole. We can see these fields and their behaviour by using iron filings.

▲ *Iron filings showing lines of force around a magnet*

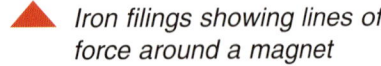

▲ *Lines of force showing that opposite poles attract each other*

▲ *Lines of force showing that similar poles repel each other*

Earth as a Magnet

The inside core of the Earth acts as a magnet. The upper part is the north pole and the bottom part is the south pole. On the crust of the Earth we also find rocks which act like magnets. These are called Lodestones.

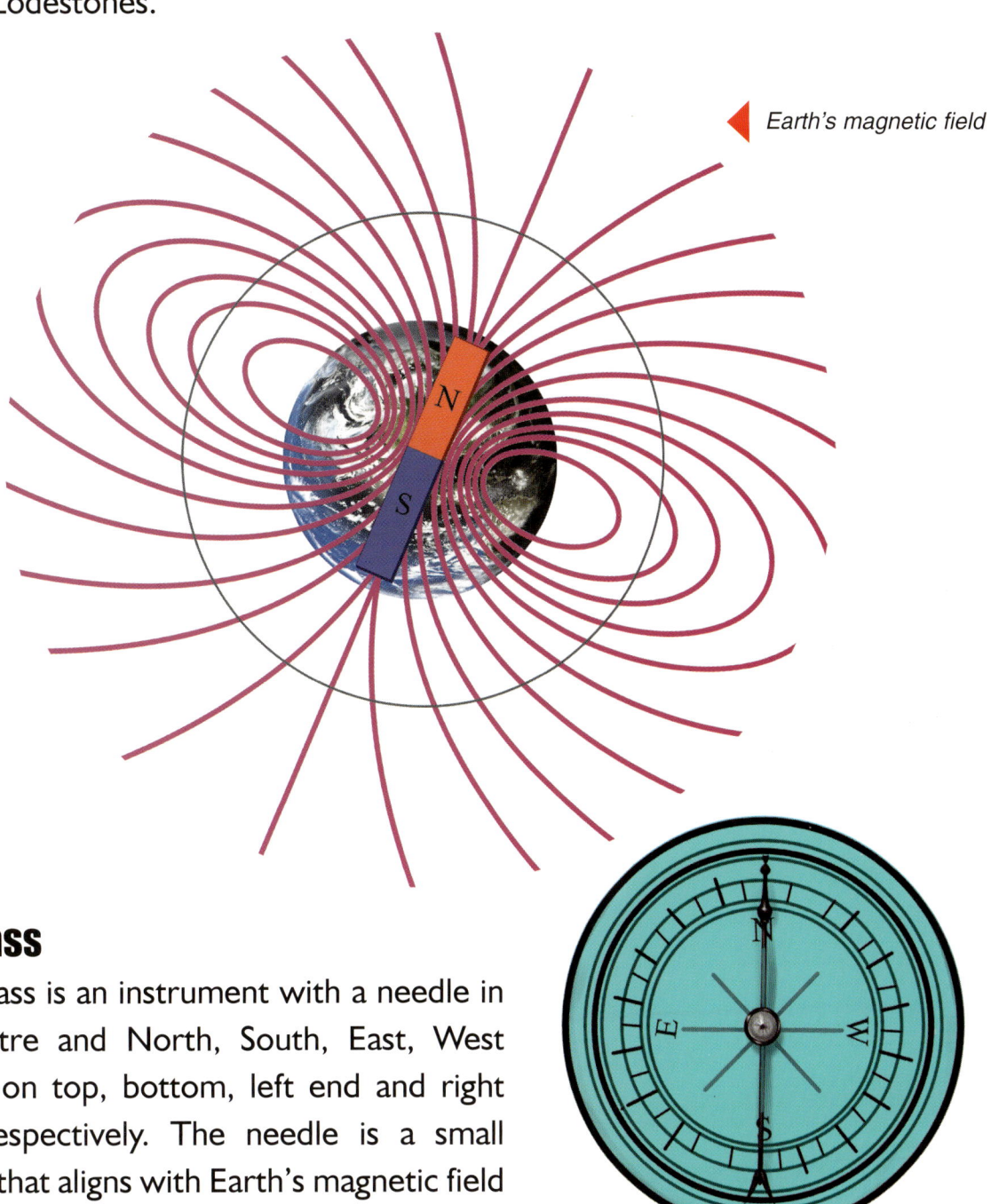

◀ Earth's magnetic field

Compass

A compass is an instrument with a needle in the centre and North, South, East, West written on top, bottom, left end and right ends, respectively. The needle is a small magnet that aligns with Earth's magnetic field and always points towards the North.

▲ Compass

Electromagnets

Electromagnets are not permanent magnets. It is that when a strong current is flowing or covering a metal, the magnetic field of that current carrying wire or coil induces magnetic properties in the metal. The moment the current is switched off the metal loses its magnetic property.

How to make a small Electromagnet

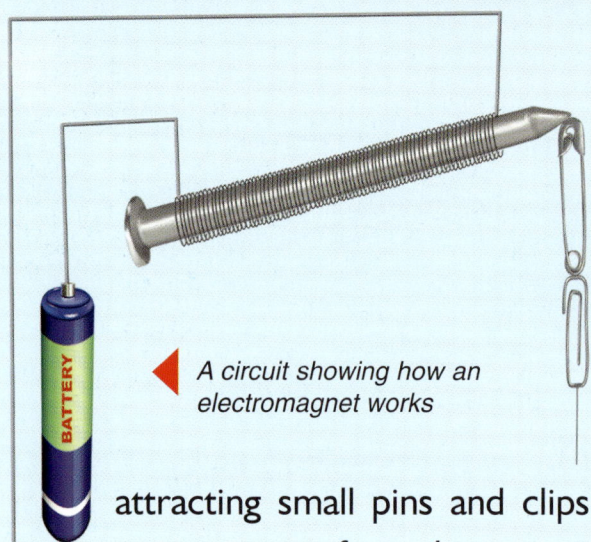

A circuit showing how an electromagnet works

Take a long iron nail and turn a wire around it to form a coil as shown in the figure. Now connect one end of the wire to the positive terminal of a regular 6 volt battery and the other end to the negative terminal. The moment the current starts flowing through the wire, your iron nail becomes a magnet and starts attracting small pins and clips of metals. (Please take help of your parents to perform this experiment or else it can be very dangerous.)

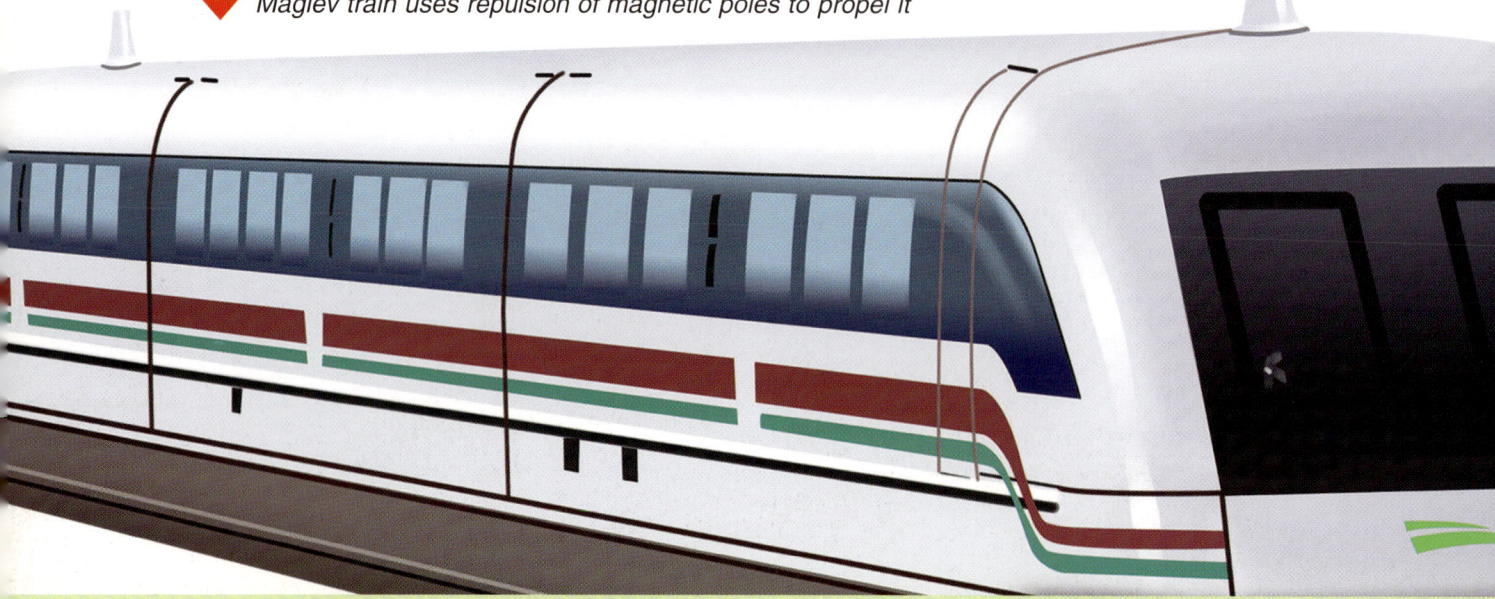

Maglev train uses repulsion of magnetic poles to propel it

Usage of Electromagnets

In our modern day life, there are huge number of applications where electromagnets are used. A huge electromagnet is used in a junk yard to separate iron, steel, and cobalt from the rest of the materials. The Maglev train uses the power of magnetic fields to propel itself. Lot of electric locomotives use electromagnets as power brakes. Even your car engine uses an electromagnetic circuit for the purpose of ignition.

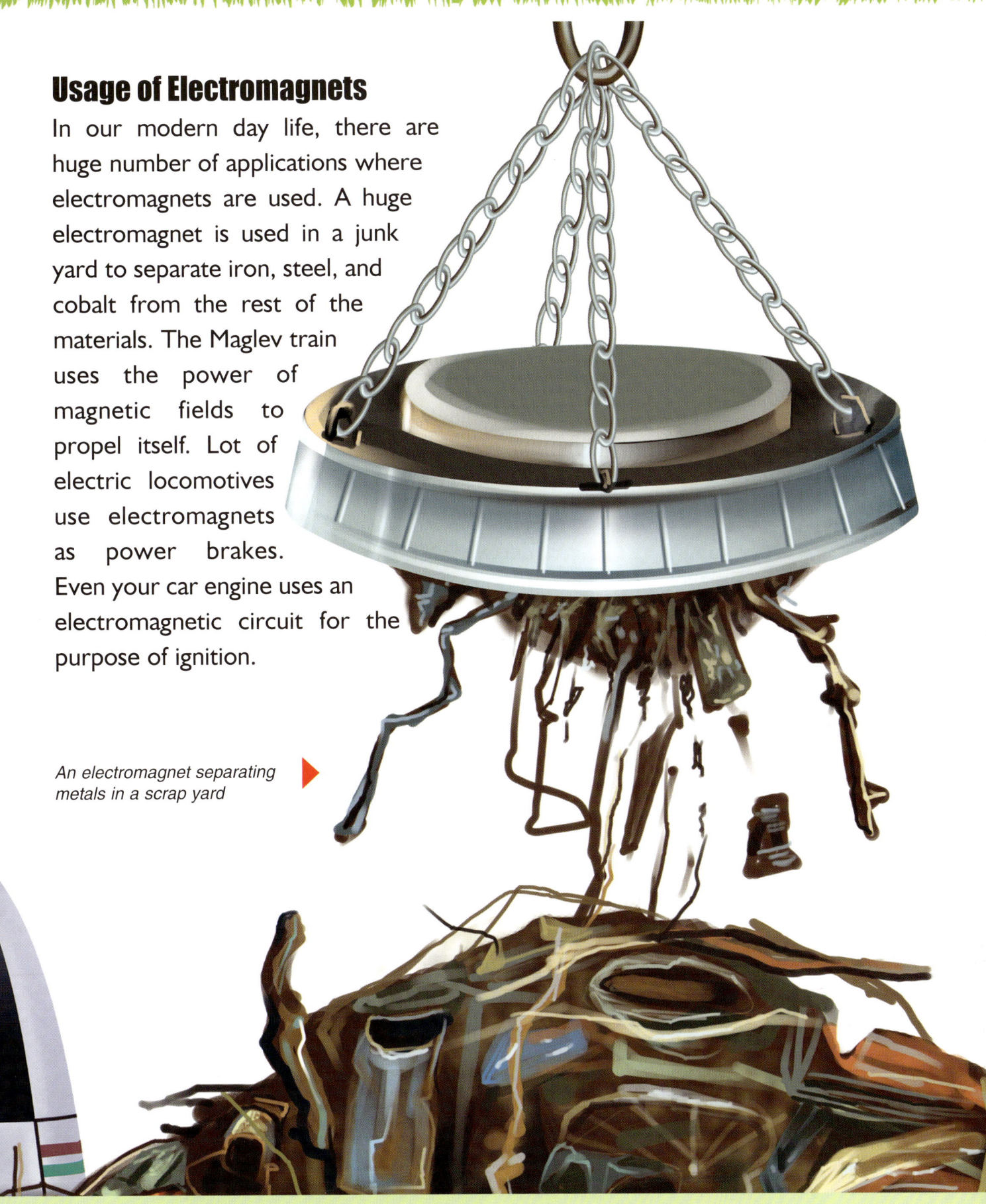

An electromagnet separating metals in a scrap yard

Classification of Living Things

There are groups in classification of livings things called Kingdoms. These classifications are done on the basis of common characteristics that living things have. There are all together five such kingdoms. Monerans, Protists, Fungi, Plants and Animals. These kingdoms are then sub-divided into Phylum and then into Class. The largest class of living things are the insects.

Monerans

These are uni-cellular organisms without a nucleus. Bacteria falls under this category.

Protists

These are uni-cellular organisms with a nucleus. Amoebae fall under this category.

▼ Monerans

▼ Protists

▼ Fungi

Mushroom and Moulds

Fungi

These are kind of organisms whose mass or body is made up of thread-like objects. Mushrooms fall under this category.

Plants

Plants are well known for making their own food with the help of sunlight. The cells of plants are unique from those of animals, as they have cell walls. Ferns, mosses, big trees all fall under this category.

Animals

These are huge multi-cellular beings found on land, water and air. Animals can move but they depend on plants and other animals for food. Birds, mammals, fishes, insects all fall under this category.

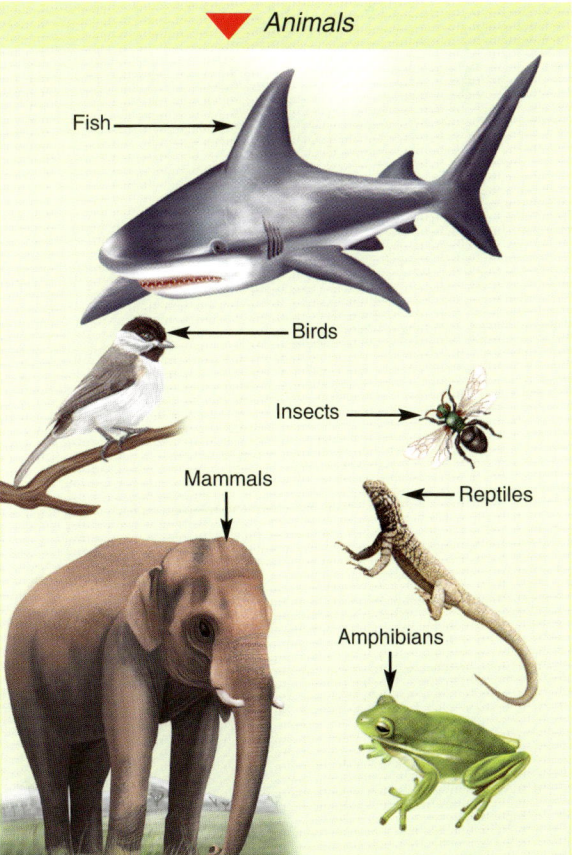

Plants and Animals

Photosynthesis

As all living things need energy (food) to live and grow, plants are the only living things which can make their own food. A plant uses the sunlight from the Sun, Carbon-dioxide from the air and water from the soil to create energy or food for its growth and hence life. This process is called photosynthesis. The green substance called chlorophyll helps the plant to make its food from natural resources.

Carnivorous Plants

Though photosynthesis helps plants make their own food, some plants need extra nutrients to grow. These plants have the capability of trapping and extracting food from small animals or insects. They come in various sizes, shapes and characteristics. One such plant is called the Venus Flytrap. When an insect sits on the sensitive leaves of this plant, it shuts instantly and through its porous cells it takes all the nutrients it requires from the insect.

Important Plants

Plants play a very important role in our ecosystem. Without plants the Earth would be a barren dry land. They help preserve soil, provide shelter, pump in fresh air or oxygen in the atmosphere. Most importantly they are the major source of food for most of the animals. Human beings, through sheer intelligence, have also discovered other useful plant products. Few of them are listed here.

Invertebrates

This is the largest group of animals found in the animal kingdom. An Invertebrate means an animal without a vertebra, or one can simply say backbone. Insects are the largest group among invertebrates. Most of the sea animals like Coral, Man O'war, Sponges are all invertebrates.

Amphibians

Amphibians comprise that category of vertebrates that can live both on land and in water. This is the smallest group among vertebrates. Amphibians though enjoy land, but they breed in water.

Mammals

Mammals are warm blooded animals and directly produce their young ones in their wombs. They also produce their own milk. Mostly they are land animals but few species are also found in the ocean.

Insects

Insects are the largest group of invertebrates. Most insects have a common body plan — the head, the thorax and the abdomen. The head has its eyes, antenna, mouth. The thorax has legs and wings if it is a flying insect and the abdomen has the stomach and the excretory system.

Vertebrates

Another group of animals, which have a backbone are called vertebrates. Fishes were the first vertebrates which came into existence. Other than fish, mammals, amphibians, reptiles are other categories in this group.

Reptiles

Reptiles is that category of vertebrates which moves on its belly. They are coldblooded animals with a scaly body. They have short legs and a tail. Most of the reptiles have an internal fertilisation system and lay eggs.

Birds

They are the largest group of warm blooded animals which lay eggs. Their body is mostly covered with feathers. Though all the birds have wings, few are flightless.

Human Anatomy

Human beings are the most intelligent out of the whole lot in the animal kingdom. They are also the only completely vertical animals. The study of the human anatomy can be divided into four categories. The cells, the tissues, the organs and the systems.

Cells

It is the smallest physical entity performing its individual independent function. It has one or more nucleii surrounded by a cell membrane.

▲ *Complex structure of a cell*

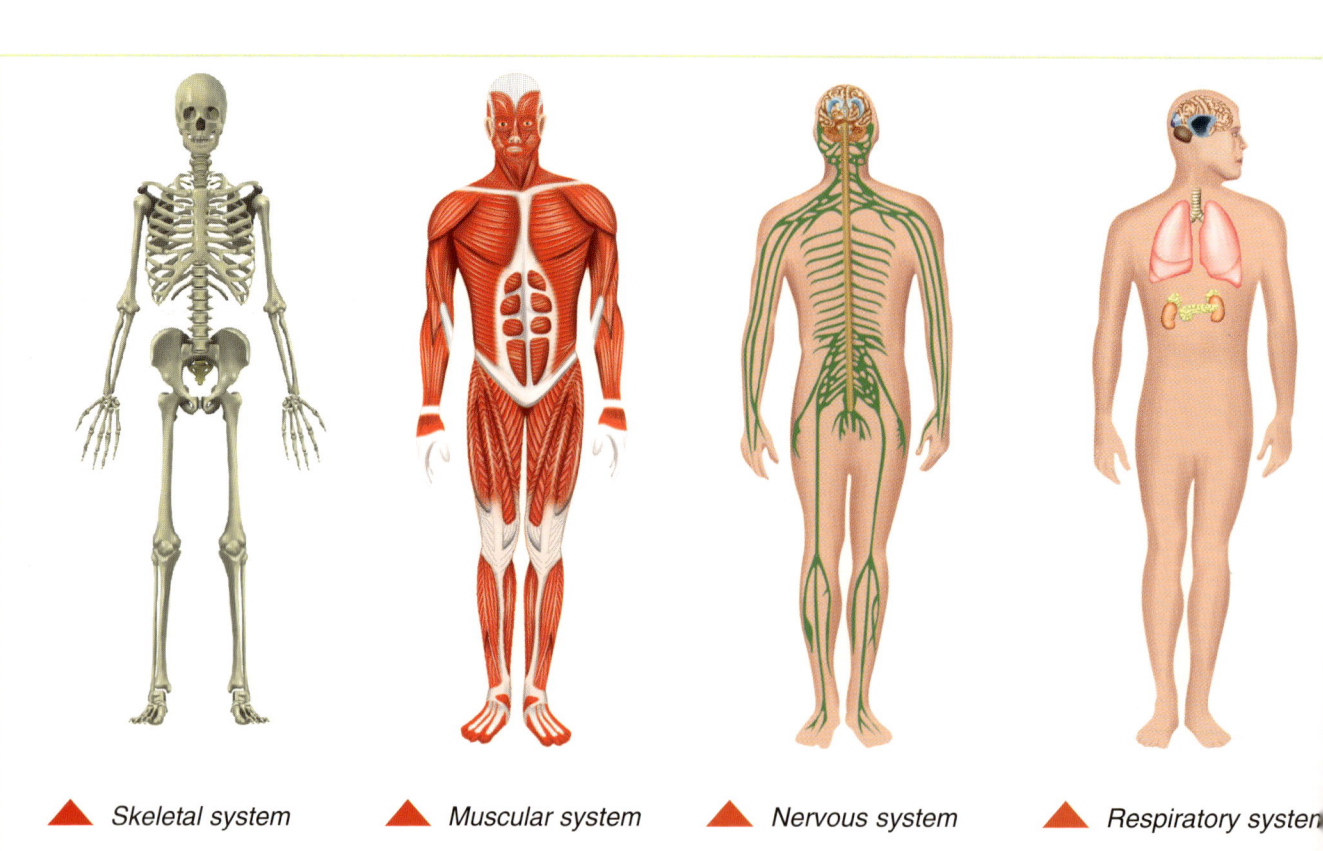

▲ *Skeletal system*　　▲ *Muscular system*　　▲ *Nervous system*　　▲ *Respiratory system*

Tissues

Tissues are a bundle of similar cells combined together to perform a particular function in our body. They are Nerve, Muscle, Epidermal and Connective.

Organs

It is a differentiated part in our body that either in full or in part consists of a particular functional unit or performs a function. For example, eyes perform the function of sight, whereas liver performs only a part of digestion.

▲ Microscopic view of a tissue

Few important human organs ▶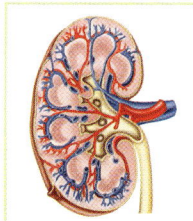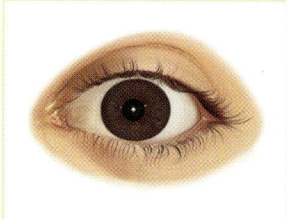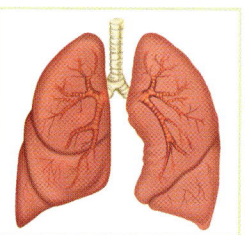

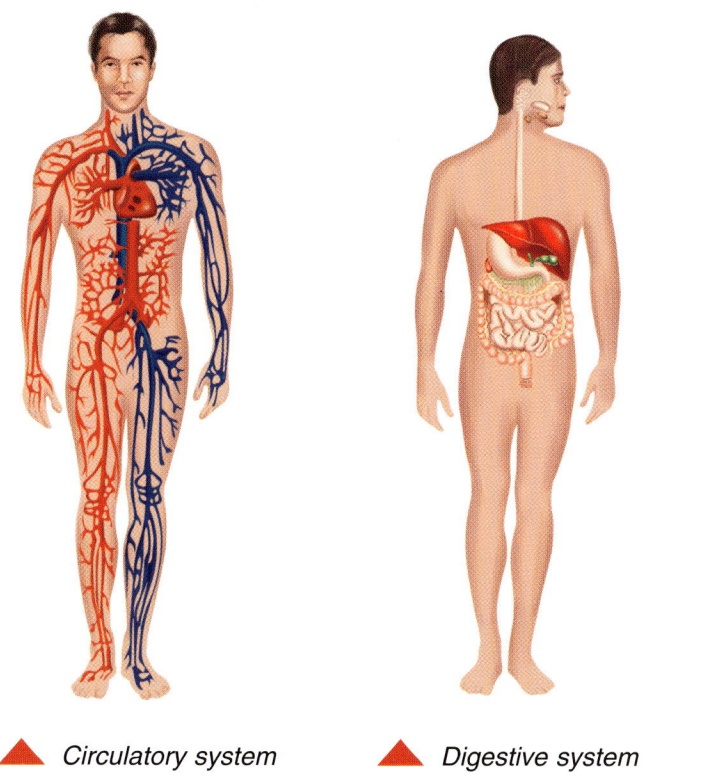

▲ Circulatory system   ▲ Digestive system

Systems

These are a whole set of functions that in totality take care of one or more processes needed by the body. The major systems in the body are: Skeletal System, Muscular System, Nervous System, Respiratory System, Digestive system, Circulatory System, Reproductive System and Excretory System.

Inventions

Early Inventions

It is said that man is the most intelligent being on planet Earth. Therefore, from the very beginning he has rationalised the very necessities and thus invention began. For almost more than 2 million years human beings have been inventing one or the other thing, as and when they have faced challenges.

Early wheel ▶

Wheel

It is not the first but definitely one of the most important inventions for mankind. Nobody knows who or when the first wheel was invented. But around 5,500 years ago, archeologists found the oldest ever evidence of the wheel. It was buried in what was known as Mesopotamia. Then onwards the wheel has really gone through many improvements and is now used for various purposes.

Fire

It is not that human beings had not seen a fire before they actually lit one. It is also difficult to say how they lit fire — it could be by rubbing two dry bamboos or by striking two stones on a small pile of dried hay. The invention of fire changed the way of life for the early man.

◀ *Early man lighting fire*

Tools

The early man found it difficult to hunt animals with his bare hands. This challenge might have led him to invent the first tool. The early tools were mostly made up of stones such as flint. Then almost 7,500 years ago metals were discovered and man started using metals to make more effective tools.

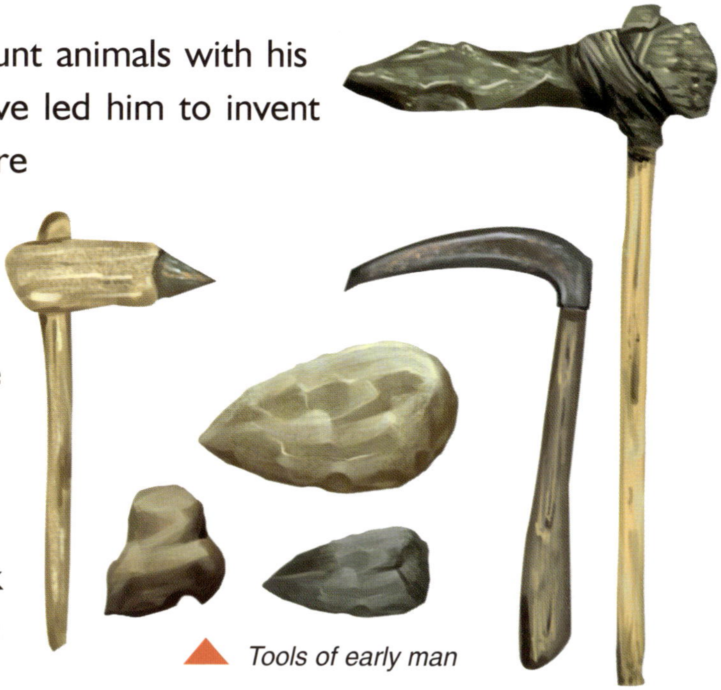

▲ Tools of early man

Archimedes' Screw

Way back in 250 odd BC, a Greek mathematician, Archimedes invented a mechanical machine to lift water. This was called Archimedes' Screw. A thin rod in the centre and screw design on it, fixed in a long barrel, was submerged in a pond as shown in the figure. The handle of the rod then rotated the water from the pond which was at a lower level, raising it up through the barrel, and collecting it on the ground.

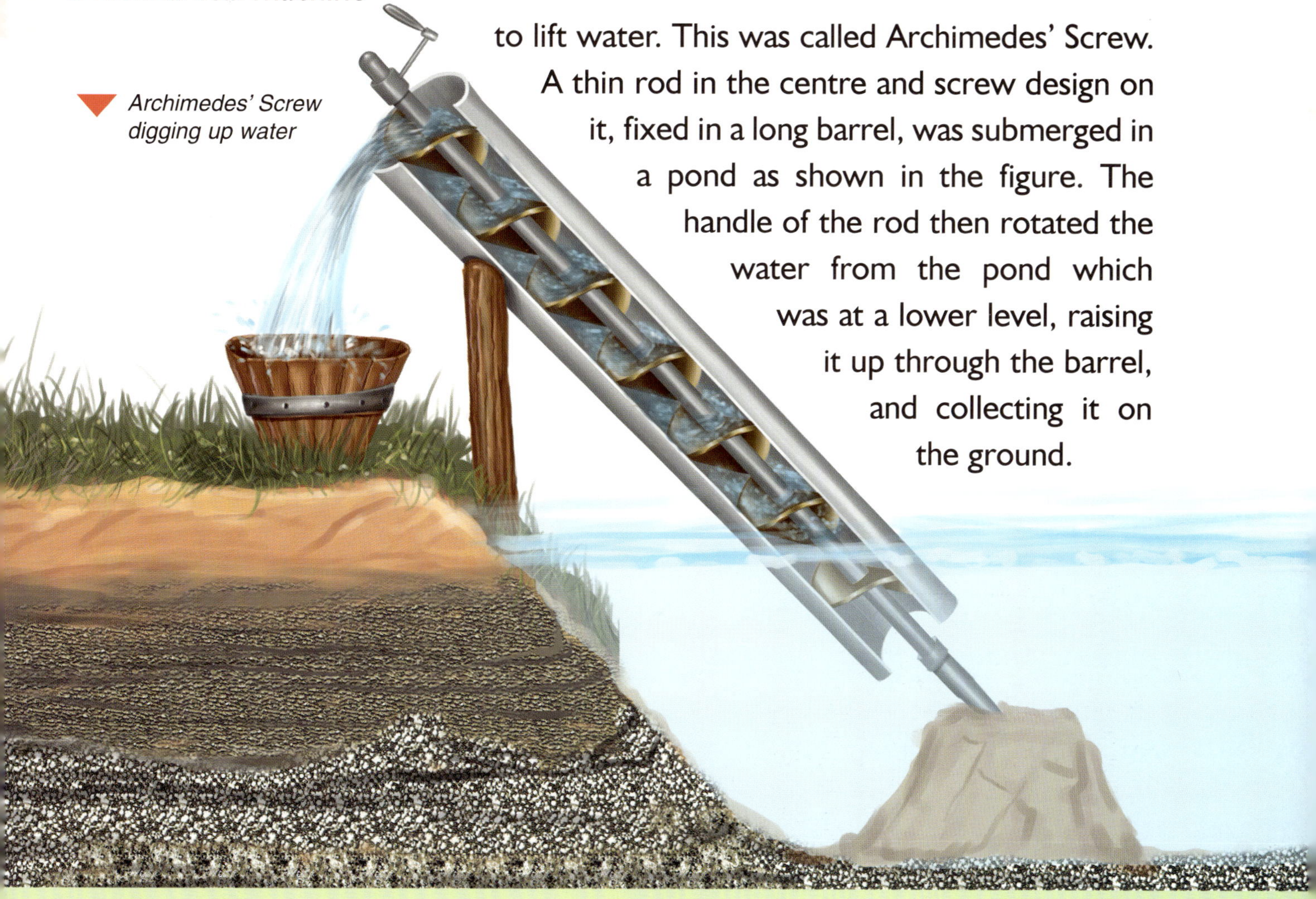

▼ Archimedes' Screw digging up water

Modern Inventions

▲ James Watt's improved steam engine

Steam Engine

Though Scottish engineer James Watt is considered to be the inventor of the steam engine, Thomas Savery, an English engineer, designed a crude steam engine in 1698. James Watt later in the 1760's improved the design and made a more efficient engine. It was such a great success that even in factories and mines, James Watt's steam engine was used to power machines.

Spinning Wheel

Almost about 1,000 years ago the spinning wheel was invented in India. Later on at the time of the Industrial Revolution, one Englishman James Hargreaves made his Spinning Jenny. From hand held single spindle spinning, he made his machine to hold multiple spindles that were rotated by turning a single wheel. Thus the single rotation enabled threads to be spun by twisting fibres together very fast.

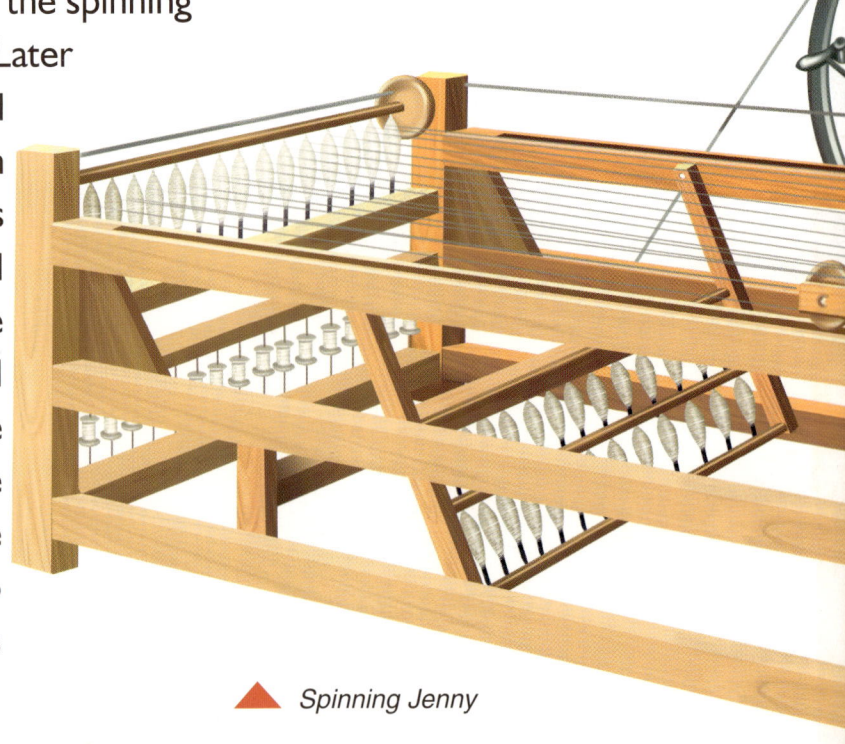

▲ Spinning Jenny

The first Electric Bulb

Though the idea of using electricity to light up was not new but till 1879 there was no practical evidence of such an invention. In 1879, Thomas Edison, after several experiments, invented the first successful Electric Bulb. It was a vaccum glass bulb where electricity was flown through a carbonised filament, and the bulb got lit as the carbonised filament glowed. Before this, lots of other threads were used by Edison to make his electric bulb. He even used threads of rubber and silk.

▼ *Thomas Edison in his workshop inventing an electrical bulb*

Transport

Stephenson's Rocket

In the 1820's Robert Stephenson floated his locomotive manufacturing company. Very soon he proved to the world that the locomotive can also be used as a passenger transport. He developed a locomotive 'Rocket' and rail travel was introduced to mankind. Rocket had the power to carry hundreds of passengers. He later also developed boiler designs.

First Passenger Train

An English engineer, George Stephenson first showed the world that a steam engine can carry passengers also. Before this, these engines were only used to carry coal. In 1830, he himself opened the first passenger rail.

Stepenson's Rocket which was used to carry passengers

▼ Wright Brothers' Biplane

Wright Brothers' Biplane

Wilbur and Oliver Wright, popularly known as the Wright Brothers, used to observe how birds would fly. They noticed that the curve in their wings supported their lift and the change in the position and shape of the wing and its feathers used to control their direction. Based on this logic they created their first Biplane in the early 1900's. This was the first successful human flight that anybody witnessed. After almost 2 years they developed the first flying machine or what we call a fixed wing aircraft.

Egyptian Sailboat

In around 4000 BC Egyptians pioneered the sail boats. These boats used to have square sail and were steered by two oars. These boats were wide enough to take weight and give stability in deep water.

▲ Egyptian sailboat

Great Scientists

Pythagoras

Pythagoras of Samos was a Greek mathematician. Though much is not known about him, he is famous for his 'Pythagoras Theorem'. This theorem is a theory of geometry which tells the size of a third line in a right triangle if one knows the size of the other two sides.

Hippocrates

It was the age when society thought that illness was caused by evil spirits. Hippocrates, an ancient Greek doctor, first revealed that illness is physically caused and happens due to unhealthy diet and environment. He is also called the Father of Medicine.

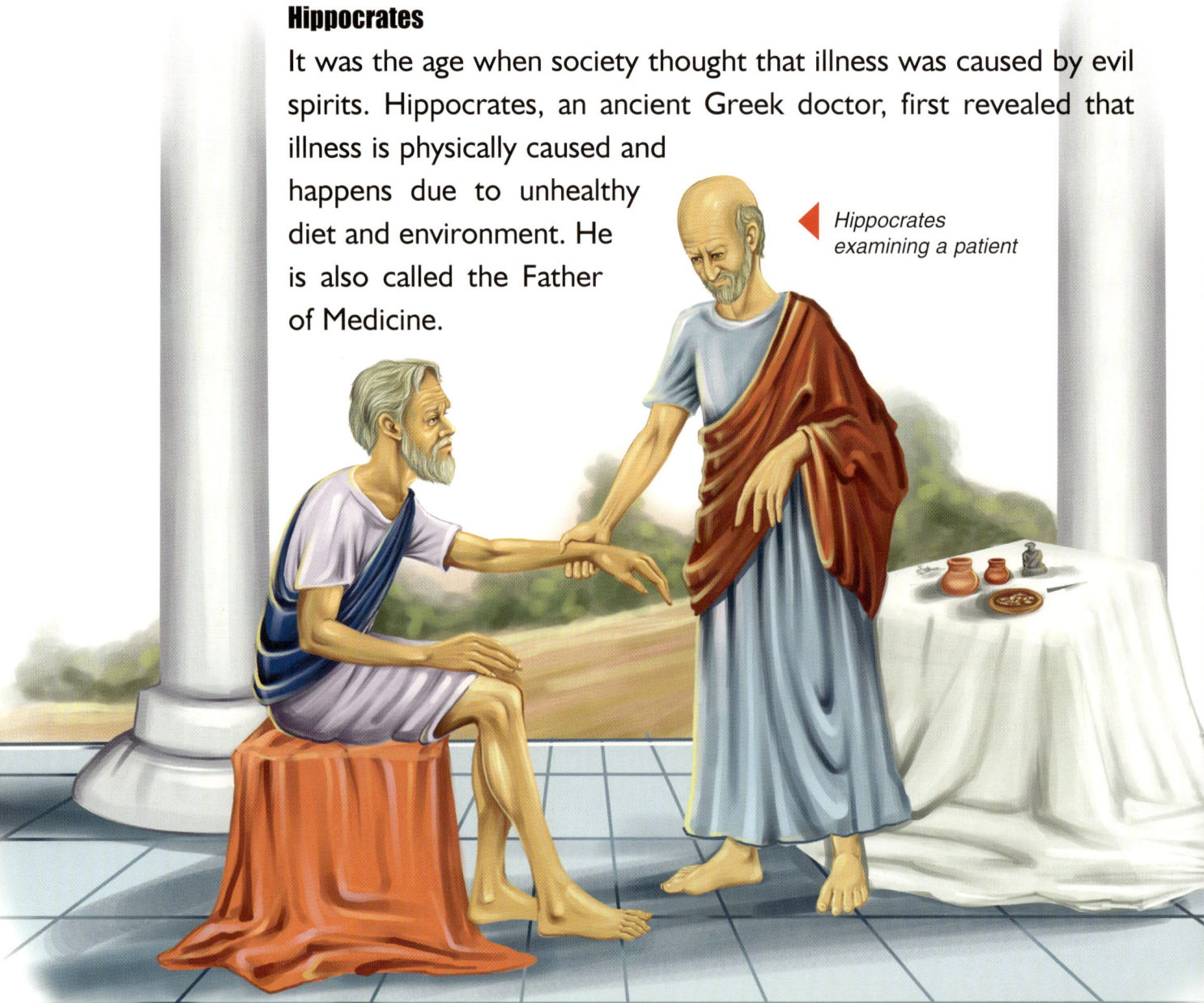

Hippocrates examining a patient

Leonardo da Vinci

He is more popular as a Renaissance artist, but the fact is, the world has still not produced a man with such diverse interests and knowledge. He was an anatomist, inventor, scientist, mathematician and so on. He has done extensive work on the human anatomy and also produced drawings of foetal study. His fascination of flight was so intense that he sketched diagrams of airplanes and helicopters. He showed the world the first machine gun drawing. Surprisingly, he also proposed a single span (approximately 720 feet) bridge. A smaller model of the same bridge was constructed in 2001, in Norway.

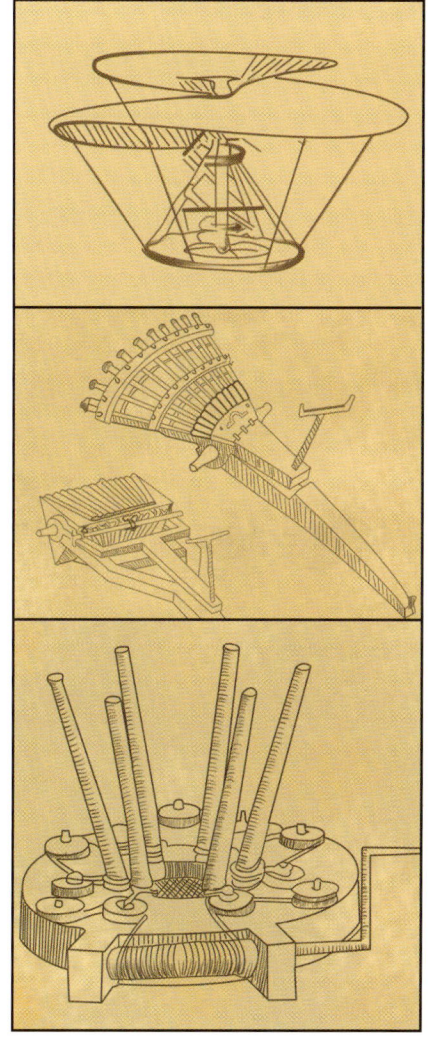

▼ *Few of Leonardo's scientific drawings*

◀ *Leonardo da Vinci*

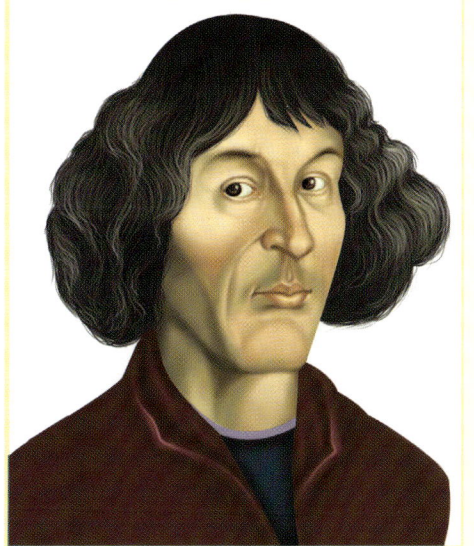

Nicolaus Copernicus

Earlier, people accepted the theory that the Sun revolves around the Earth and other planets. It is only in the 16th century that Copernicus, a Polish astronomer, from his observations came out with his theory that the Sun is the centre of the Solar System and all the other planets revolve around it. It took almost 100 years for people to accept his theory.

Issac Newton

Newton is one of the all time great scientists ever born. He was an English mathematician and a physicist. During his lifetime he wrote many theories out of which the 'Law of Gravity' and 'Law of Motion' are the most famous. He was the first man to tell the world that an invisible force binds all matter together by pulling any object towards it. This invisible force is 'gravity'. He also discovered that light is a mixture of seven other coloured lights and called it a Spectrum.

◄ Newton watching an apple falling from a tree

Benjamin Franklin

Franklin is another very renowned scientist of the 1700's. He wondered if lightning was a kind of electricity. So to know this, he performed an experiment by flying a kite on a stormy night. He tied a metallic key with the thread of the kite and when lightning happened the key sparked brightly. He discovered that lightning is basically electricity. He also invented the lightning rod, bifocals and Franklin Stove.

Charles Darwin

He was an English naturalist, who very early in life, became popular amongst the scientific community with his work in the field of geology. He provided scientific proof that all species of life have evolved over a time from ancestors through the process of natural selection. Later he extended his theory to 'Survival of the Fittest'. It was only in the 1930's that his theory of natural selection came into wide acceptance not only by the biologists, but also by the masses.

▲ *Charles Darwin*

Albert Einstein

Einstein was a Germany based Jewish physicist who is also called the Father of Physics. He was honoured with the Nobel Prize in Physics in 1921. He enlightened the world that time is not a direction that flows from past to future but is basically a dimension. It means it is relative. This is called the 'Theory of Relativity.' Another of his major theories is about the conversion of mass into energy, or $E = MC^2$. This theory led to the invention of the atom bomb.

◀ *Sir Albert Einstein*

Reprinted in 2015

An imprint of Om Books International

Corporate & Editorial Office
A 12, Sector 64, Noida 201 301
Uttar Pradesh, India
Phone: +91 120 477 4100
Email: editorial@ombooks.com
Website: www.ombooksinternational.com

Sales Office
107, Ansari Road, Darya Ganj, New Delhi 110 002, India
Phone: +91 11 4000 9000, 2326 3363, 2326 5303
Fax: +91 11 2327 8091
Email: sales@ombooks.com
Website: www.ombooks.com

Copyright © Om Books International 2010

Art Editor: Rachna Panchal

ALL RIGHTS RESERVED. No part of this book may be reproduced or transmitted in any form by any means, electronic or mechanical, including photocopying and recording, or by any information storage and retrieval system, except as may be expressly permitted in writing by the publisher.

ISBN: 978-81-87108-95-5

Printed in India

10 9 8 7 6 5 4 3 2